SQUADRONS!

No. 1

THE SUPERMARINE
SPITFIRE MK. VI

PHIL H. LISTEMANN

ISBN: 978-2918590-38-5

Copyright

© 2013 Philedition - Phil Listemann

revised Jun.2015, Dec.2018, Oct.2021

Colour profiles: Gaetan Marie/Bravo Bravo Aviation

All right reserved. No part of this book may be reproduced, stored in a retrieval system or transmitted in any form by any means, electronic, mechanical, photocopying, recording or otherwise, without prior permission of the author.

GLOSSARY OF TERMS

PERSONEL :

(AUS)/RAF: Australian serving in the RAF
(BEL)/RAF: Belgian serving in the RAF
(CAN)/RAF: Canadian serving in the RAF
(CZ)/RAF: Czechoslovak serving in the RAF
(NFL)/RAF: Newfoundlander serving in the RAF
(NL)/RAF: Dutch serving in the RAF
(NZ)/RAF: New Zealander serving in the RAF
(POL)/RAF: Pole serving in the RAF
(RHO)/RAF: Rhodesian serving in the RAF
(SA)/RAF: South African serving in the RAF
(US)/RAF - RCAF : American serving in the RAF or RCAF

RANKS

G/C : Group Captain
W/C : Wing Commander
S/L : Squadron Leader
F/L : Flight Lieutenant
F/O : Flying Officer
P/O : Pilot Officer
W/O : Warrant Officer
F/Sgt : Flight Sergeant
Sgt : Sergeant
Cpl : Corporal
LAC : Leading Aircraftman

OTHER

ATA: Air Transport Auxiliary
CO : Commander
DFC : Distinguished Flying Cross
DFM : Distinguished Flying Medal
DSO : Distinguished Service Order
Eva. : Evaded
ORB : Operational Record Book
OTU : Operational Training Unit
PoW : Prisoner of War
PAF: Polish Air Force
RAF : Royal Air Force
RAAF : Royal Australian Air Force
RCAF : Royal Canadian Air Force
RNZAF : Royal New Zealand Air Force
SAAF : South African Air Force
s/d: Shot down
Sqn : Squadron
† : Killed

CODENAMES - OFFENSIVE OPERATIONS - FIGHTER COMMAND

CIRCUS:
Bombers heavily escorted by fighters, the purpose being to bring enemy fighters into combat.

RAMROD:
Bombers escorted by fighters, the primary aim being to destroy a target.

RANGER:
Large formation freelance intrusion over enemy territory with aim of wearing down enemy fighters.

RHUBARB:
Freelance fighter sortie against targets of opportunity.

ROADSTEAD:
Dive bombing and low level attacks on enemy ships at sea or in harbour

RODEO:
A fighter sweep without bombers.

SWEEP:
An offensive flight by fighters designed to draw up and clear the enemy from the sky.

THE SPITFIRE MK VI

When the RAF was looking for high-altitude fighter, thoughts naturally turned to the Spitfire to fulfil this role. This requirement eventually gave rise to the Supermarine Type 350, or Spitfire Mk.VI. The Mk.VI was basically a Spitfire Mk.V airframe with a pressurised cockpit, allied to a Rolls-Royce Merlin 47. (The Merlin 49 was originally planned for this version, but did not go into production).

The first prototype for the Mk.VI was Spitfire R7120 which combined both the pressurised cockpit and the Merlin 47. It was tested by the Royal Aircraft Establishment (R.A.E.) in June 1941. A second conversion, X4942, followed, and was widely seen as the true prototype of the Mk.VI version because it had extended wing-tips, which R7120 did not. X4942 made its first flight on 4 July, while R7120 first flew on 25 August.

Tests were carried out over the succeeding weeks, and 100 Spitfire Mk.VIs were ordered by amending contracts already underway, with the completion of delivery requested for June 1942. The performance of the Mk.VI was very close to that of the Mk.VB, but the Mk.VI was able to fly much higher with a service ceiling of 40,000 feet instead of 36,200 for the Mk.VB. The Mk.VI was also heavier by about 170 lb, largely owing to the pressurisation system, but also due to its pointed wing tips. These wing tips and the four-blade propellers made the identification of a Mk.VI easy on the ground.

While 100 Spitfire Mk.VIs were ordered, only 98 are actually recorded as being built to that standard and these were delivered between January and November 1942:

January 1942: AB200, AB503 **(2)**.
February 1942: AB176 (converted from a Mk.VB), AB211, AB498, AB506, AB513, AB516, AB523, AB527, AB528, BR189 **(10)**.
March 1942 : AB530, AB534, BR159, BR162, BR164, BR167, BR171, BR174, BR178, BR181, BR186, BR189, BR191, BR193 **(14)**.
April 1942 : AB529, AB533, BR172, BR197, BR200, BR205, BR243, BR247, BR250, BR252, BR255, BR286, BR287, BR289, BR297, BR298, BR304, BR326 **(18)**.
May 1942: BR302, BR307, BR309, BR310, BR314, BR318, BR319, BR329, BR330, BR563, BR567, BR569, BR571, BR575, BR577, BR579 **(16)**.
June 1942: BR578, BR585, BR587, BR588, BR590, BR593, BR595, BR597, BR598, BR599, BR979 **(11)**.
July 1942: BR983, BR984, BR987, BS106, BS108, BS111, BS114, BS115, BS117, BS124 **(10)**.
August 1942: BS133, BS134, BS141, BS146, BS149, BS427 **(6)**.
September 1942: BS436, BS437, BS442 **(3)**.
October 1942: BS228, BS245, BS448, BS453, BS460, BS465, BS472 **(7)**.
November 1942: EN176, EN189 **(2)**.

Counting the two experimental conversions, R7120 and X4942, there were a total of 99 Spitfires which are known to have the Mk.VI classification applied to them. Of the production aircraft, all but one (BR250) were used by operational units. Although the Mk.VI was intended for UK use only, five were shipped to the Middle East and the Mk.VI was mainly used by two RAF Fighter Command units, 124 and 616 Squadrons, between July 1942 and September 1943. Nine other fighter squadrons were partially or totally equipped with this type. However, these units were usually based far from any area of enemy activity. The use of the Mk.VI in the latter case can be seen as a cheap way to maintain the skills of fighter pilots during periods of rest, to give them a good training in a high altitude fighter, and to be present in case of incursions by high-flying German reconnaissance aircraft over Scotland. The Mk. VI found also a great utility for some reconnaissance squadrons or for Meteorological Reconnaissance ('Met') units where the Mk.VI's ability to fly at high altitudes gave valuable service.

Generally speaking the Mk.VI was unpopular with both pilots and engine fitters due to its pressurisation system. The impact of the Mk.VI on the wartime career of the Spitfire was negligible, with around 5,000 fighter sorties. Of these, 90% were carried out by 124 and 616 squadrons, during which fewer than 20 victories (confirmed or probable) were claimed, against 24 aircraft lost in operations – one quarter of the entire production. By 1945, around 30 remained in RAF charge, most being in store. From February 1945, they began to be struck off charge, batch by batch, and by VE-Day, only BR250 in UK was still officially on the RAF's books. It was eventually struck off charge on 19 October.

Side view of the AB200 early in 1942. AB200 was the first production Mk.VI. It was used for various tests the next 18 months, and served with No.124 Sqn at the really end of its flying career. It was stored from October 1943 onwards and seems not to have flown again. No struck off charge date is available, but it was probably scrapped before the end of war.
(P. Arnold's collection)

Two views of X4942, the second Spitfire modified as an Mk.VI, which is seen as the first true prototype. Above with the three-blade propeller and below with a four-blade propeller. X4942 became maintenance airframe in November 1943 as 4264M. (*P. Arnold's collection*)

Another view of X4942 in flight. This Spitfire was built as a Mk.I and converted to Mk.VA and never entered RAF service. As the photograph is showing, only guns were installed on Mk.VA version unlike the production Mk.VIs derivated from Mk.VB with 20mm cannons. *(P. Arnold's collection)*

July 1942
May 1943

Victories - confirmed or probable claims: 13.0

First operational sortie: 28.07.42
Last operational sortie: 30.05.43

Number of sorties: ca. 1,070
Total aircraft written-off: 10
Aircraft lost on operations: 6
Aircraft lost in accidents: 4

Squadron code letters:
ON

Commanding Officers

S/L Thomas Balmforth	RAF No. 41363	RAF	...	18.12.42
S/L James C. Nelson	RAF No. 100525	(US)/RAF	18.12.42	...

Squadron Usage

Number 124 Squadron had been flying Spitfires for about a year when it was selected to fly the Mk.VI. In that time it had claimed around 10 victories and counted a number of experienced pilots in its ranks, including the newly promoted CO. Thomas Balmforth was a long serving pilot with the squadron, and had recently been awarded the DFC.

The least that can be said is that the arrival of the Mk.VI did not provoke any particular comment from the pilots. The last sorties on the Mk.V were carried out on the 25 July, and the first on the Mk.VI, a squadron sweep to Fecamp led by the CO, was conducted three days later. The squadron patrolled at 19,000 feet without incident. Two days later, 124 Squadron was sent with 616 Squadron to cover the withdrawal of 41 and 71 (Eagle) Squadrons from the Cap-Gris-Nez/Boulogne area, once again without incident, the altitude reached being 17,000 feet. The Squadron did not fly in operations again for a fortnight, despite being at readiness on occasion during this period. On 17 August, a major operation, *Circus* 204, took place. This was an attack on the marshalling yards at Rouen, but 124 Squadron was only required to act as a diversion. After one day's rest, the Squadron participated in Operation Jubilee, over Dieppe. The day started early with a patrol over Dieppe anchorage between 04.45 and 06.22, led by W/C R.M.B.D. Duke-Wolley. The Squadron orbited over the target for 30 minutes

When 124 received its first Spitfire VI, Tommy Balmforth had been just promoted to command the squadron. He joined the RAF in October 1938 and when war broke out he was tasked to ferry aircraft between RAF stations. This task led him to ferry Hurricanes in the Middle East in June 1940. His travel was stopped at Malta and was attached to the Fighter Flight which was raised into No. 261 Squadron in August. In January 1941 he was however evacuated to the UK due to ill health. He joined 124 Squadron in September 1941 and was awarded the DFC in May 1942. He was rested in January 1943 but would return in June to lead the squadron again until September 1944, this time to fly Spitfire Mk VIIs. In October 1944 he became Wing Leader at Manston, a position he left in December 1944. He was made Companion of the DSO in April 1945.

Albert Herreman was the only Belgian pilot to have claimed a 'kill' on a German aircraft while flying a Spitfire Mk.VI. He enlisted in the Belgian military aviation in March 1940 before moving with his unit to France then French Morocco, eventually arriving in Great Britain in August 1940. He completed his training as a fighter pilot and joined No.123 Sqn in October 1941 and the following month, No.124 Sqn. In September 1942, he was posted to No.350 (Belgian) Sqn and was commissioned the following March. Herreman did not survive the war, being killed in action on 8 June 1944.
(André Bar)

without seeing any action. A second sortie took place late in the morning between 10.49 and 12.20.

A rendezvous was made with 616 Squadron over the Channel off Beachy Head, before the Squadrons climbed to 10,000 feet in the Dieppe area. Enemy aircraft were seen and attacked and F/L W. Gregson was able to claim a Fw190 as damaged, soon followed by another one as destroyed. At the same time, F/Sgt P.E.G. Durnford attacked another Fw190 from 200 yards and then, after having fired a second burst, saw the Fw190 start smoking and then catch fire. The Fw190 was claimed as probable only, but was later confirmed as destroyed by Fighter Command. Later, while flying at 5,000 feet over Dieppe, Durnford saw a Ju88 (later identified as a Do217) flying 3,000 ft below him and dived in order to close to 300 yards. The bomber had also dived, to fly at top-tree level. This was not enough, however, to save itself, and Balmforth fired a burst which set the left engine on fire. The crew jettisoned its bombs and crashed into a field. This bomber was claimed as destroyed. During in the same period, P/O M.P. Kilburn claimed a Fw190 as probable. This success, however was not one-sided, as Sgt J.B. Shanks had to make a forced landing near Dieppe following a dogfight with German fighters and became a PoW. On the third sortie (13.20-15.00), the Squadron was again successful, especially P/O B.J. Hull who was able to claim one Fw190 destroyed, another one as damaged and one Ju88 as probably destroyed within a single minute, while P/O A.G. Russell and F/L Gregson each claimed a Fw190 as damaged. The day ended with another patrol between 17.19 and 18.47. In all, the Squadron performed 48 sorties and claimed four confirmed victories, two probable and five damaged. The Squadron continued to carry out missions almost every day until the end of the month, most of which were uneventful other than a diversionary sweep (*Circus* 211) on the 29 August, when 124 Squadron added two more victories to its tally – one Fw190 destroyed by the Belgian pilot A. Herreman, and another by P/O Kilburn. The German fighters had been engaged six miles NW of Cap Gris-Nez, at between 25,000 and 27,000 feet.

Other than the tragic loss of a Canadian pilot, Sgt J. Shea on 28th during a training flight when he was unable to recover from a spin, September was rather quiet, with only 77 sorties being carried out. October, however, was a busy month with over 350 sorties, and would remain the most prolific month in the Squadron's Mk.VI era. This did not create more opportunities for the pilots to make

Michael P. 'Slim' Kilburn was a Londener of Irish parentage and was posted to No.124 Sqn as first assignment in May 1941 and when the first Spitfire Mk.VIs arrived at the Squadron he was one of the most successful pilots of the 124. He flew regularly on BR579/ON-H with which he made all his claims on this mark.

Combat report:
A. Herreman (Belgian), 29 August 1942

FORM "F"   SECRET
FIGHTER COMMAND COMBAT REPORT.

From:—

- (A) Sector Serial No. ....
- (B) Serial No. of Order detailing Flight or Squadron to patrol ....
- (C) Date .... 29/8/42.
- (D) Flight .... "B".   Squadron .... 124(Baroda). Squadron.
- (E) Number of Enemy Aircraft .... 3.
- (F) Type of Enemy Aircraft .... F.W.190's
- (G) Time attack was delivered .... 11.00 hours approx.
- (H) Place attack was delivered .... 1 mile off Gris Nez
- (J) Height of Enemy .... 8/10,000 feet.
- (K) Enemy Casualties .... 1 F.W.190 ~~damaged~~ destroyed.
- (L) Our Casualties—Aircraft .... Nil
- (M) " " Personnel .... Nil
- (N) (i) Searchlights (Did they illuminate enemy; if not, were they in front or behind enemy?) .... N/A
  - (ii) Anti-aircraft guns (Did shell bursts assist pilot in intercepting the enemy?) .... N/A
- (P) Range at which fire was opened in each attack on the enemy, together with estimated length of burst .... 300 - 250 2/3 secs. m.g.
- (R) GENERAL REPORT :—

    I was flying Red 3 when at 11.00 hours Red 1 attacked three F.W.190's. I opened fire, machine guns only, at one of them (2 to 3 sec. bursts 300 to 250 yards). It turned on its back and dived down. At the same moment I was obliged to break away being attacked by 2 F.W.190's diving out sun. Later it was seen by Red 1 and 2 going down leaving a trail of black smoke.

              Signed Sergt. Herreman (Belgian)
              124 Squadron.

                        P.T.O.

R.A.F. Form 1151.

BR579/ON-H seen from an interesting angle. Note the large cabin air intake, part of the pressure system uner the pipes. It is another way to identify a Mk.VI, like the four-blade propeller. Worth noting, just before the cockpit, the name 'Boroda' from the surname of the Squadron has been partially over painted.

Two young New Zealanders joined 124 Sqn late 1942, while operating the Mk.VI, left, Bruce McK. Hirstich who was killed in action after a couple of sorties only, and right, Keith Noble-Campbell who later was made B Flight Commander in 1945. Note the Silver Fern on his breast pocket, identifying him as a New Zealander.
(Hirtich family and Keith Noble-Campbell)

more claims, though. Only one claim was made that month, on the 2 October, during a return escort of American Fortresses from St-Omer. P/O Durnford (now commissioned), scored hits on a Fw190 which was claimed as a probable. Otherwise, training continued during the month, sometime with disastrous results. On the 15th, while practising formation flying, BR567, flown by Sgt E.Q. Riseley, was hit by the aircraft flown by Sgt L.C. Haynes, and Riseley was obliged to bale out from 25,000 feet.

Surprisingly, the Mk.VI was not only used as a high altitude fighter, but also used in strafing ground or maritime targets as with 'standard' Spitfire Mk.V units. An example of this occurred on 2 November, when P/O Durnford and F/O P. Haywood, returning from a weather recce over Le Havre, sighted a tanker five miles north of the town and decided to attack. Two attacks were made, anti-aircraft gunners were reported to have been killed, and the tanker was left with smoke streaming from it. On 19 November, P/O Durnford took off from Martlesham Heath at 14.25 leading three other Spitfires on a Rhubarb over the Netherlands. Intense

Desmond P. 'Neid' Kelly from Victoria, Australia was among the last pilots who were able to fly on Mk.VI in 1943, having joined the 124 in late Spring. He was later on posted to 616 Sqn and lost an eye in combat. He tried to return to operations after recovery and this was impossible. However, ironically, Kelly was one of the first Australians to fly the Meteor and became a conversion pilot at No.1335 CU. *(Brendan Kelly via Drew Harrison)*

light flight was encountered, and Durnford's aircraft was hit, forcing him to ditch two miles west of Vlissingen. His wingmen saw him entering his dinghy, but the arrival of two Fw190s prevented them from watching more of the situation. Durnford survived and spent 12 hours in his dinghy before being washed ashore on the Dutch coast. He spent the rest of the war as a PoW.

In December, bad weather prevailed for most of the month, and little operational flying was done. However on the 12th, the Squadron became part of a big mission with No. 616, the other Mk.VI Squadron, once more escorting USAAF Fortresses. The Squadron climbed to 28,000 feet, but F/L Gregson's oxygen failed on the outward trip obliging him to remain at 15,000 feet. For a time, he followed the second formation of bombers, now far from his squadron-mates. Later, the last group of bombers came up, unescorted, and Gregson decided to join them. Soon afterwards, he noticed a squadron of aircraft coming in from the north, which at first he thought were was his squadron mates... this proved to be a mistake. By the time he realised this was in fact a formation of Fw190s, the German fighters were diving into the Fortresses, the later being prompt to open fire at the Germans. Gregson decided to join in, and was able to shoot at a Fw190. However, he was soon attacked himself, and while taking evasive action, he saw the first German crashing into the sea. Gregson then called his squadron on the radio, which soon arrived to take part to the melee. P/O Hull attacked a Fw190 from astern, after which it dived into the sea, while F/L Kilburn, now a Fight Commander, attacked other aircraft, destroying one, and sharing another with Sgt J. Saphir, a young Canadian of Austrian Jewish parentage who had recently joined the squadron. The CO, S/L Balmforth also attacked a Fw190. He attacked it while he was flying at about 18,000 feet and the German fighter was 2000-3000 feet below him. The Fw190 went in a in 30-45 ° dive with S/L Balmforth behind but the latter was unable to close in despite of the height advantage. He followed the Fw190 until being at about 6,000 feet and seeing that he had no chance of closing range he fired five two-seconds bursts from dead astern and one deflection shot at a range of 800-1000 yards. The Fw190 turned on its back and dived vertically for cloud. Tommy Balmforth saw the Focke-Wulf to go through the cloud and at the saem moment he realised that he had enough altitude to pull out. So he did and then he last saw the Fw190 going vertically through the cloud. Squadron Leader Balmforth fired at it once more but too far to make hits but he thought that the Fw190 had little chance to recover form his dive. Therefore he claimed the Fw190 as a probably destroyed. The month, ended with the departure of two experienced pilots – the CO, posted to Central Gunnery School, and F/L Gregson to 58 OTU, replaced at the head of B Flight by F/L F.G.H. Chalk. Balmforth was replaced by a former American 'Eagle

Top view of BR579/ON-H exposing the wing tips.

Jimmy Nelson took over the squadron in December 1942. An American from Colorado, he served with No. 133 (Eagle) Squadron between September 1941 and September 1942. He elected not to transfer to the USAAF and continued to serve in the RAF. When he left 124, he served as a test pilot and was victim of a serious accident on 23 August 1944 while test flying a Mosquito XVI. He never totally recovered and was eventually medically discharged in April 1945.

Squadron' pilot, S/L J.C. Nelson, who had served with 133 Squadron between September 1941 and September 1942.

Bad weather in January prevented any intensive air activity, as well the fact that the Squadron was now based at Drem close to Edinburgh, and far from where the Luftwaffe was likely to be found. Two missions were, however, carried out – these were providing escorts for a cruiser on the 3rd and the 16th. On the 20th, the Squadron finally absorbed the Sub Stratosphere (SS) Flight (see relevant chapter) which had been formed to intercept the Ju86P. The Flight came with its six pilots as well as a single Mk.VI Spitfire and some Mk.IXs and Mk.VIIs, so the Squadron became larger than the average fighter unit. On the 21st, the Squadron moved south to North Weald. That day, while flying a Spitfire Mk.IX (BL639), F/L Kilburn experienced engine failure and crashed into a 124 Squadron Mk.VI, BR181, on which mechanics were working. One mechanic, LAC Clifford T. Jones, was killed. The Mk.VI was damaged beyond repair while BL639 was later repaired. As for the pilot, he escaped major injuries as did the other mechanics. The situation came to an end by the end of the month, and the extra pilots were eventually posted away as the Squadron reverted to a normal size unit.

In February, the Squadron has been notified that it was soon to receive the Mk.VII Spitfire, and the transition (mainly ground school) soon began. Operational flying was still carried out on Mk.VIs, but the Mk.VII was eagerly awaited. Besides convoy patrols, the Squadron was sometimes called for more offensive missions, such as a *Circus* sortie to St-Omer on the 4th or a *Rodeo* (No.170) on the 16th. On 17 February, the Squadron sustained one of the worst operational losses since its formation. That day, the Squadron was called to escort 12 Venturas to the Dunkirk area (*Circus* 269). However due to bad weather, the Venturas were eventually recalled, but the Squadron continued to climb to 18,000 feet when it was warned that enemy aircraft had been detected over Gravelines. The Spitfires turned for home but were caught by about 40 Fw190s, a number which soon swelled to around 60. At least one Fw190 was damaged before the Spitfires were able to disengage, but not all of them were able to make it back home. F/O B.R. Murphy was last heard on the radio indicating that he had bagged a Fw190, but failed to return. He evaded capture and was able to reach Gibraltar in August 1942 thanks to the French Resistance, and would later rejoin the Squadron. However, his claim was never reported as such. F/L 'Jerry' Chalk, the B Flight CO was last seen diving pursued by four Fw190s and was presumed to have been shot down; Chalk was unusual as he was a former Wellington pilot and had been awarded his DFC while flying with 218 Sqn in June 1941. P/O Hull reported that he had been hit, and was seen going down. Finally, Sgt B.M. Hirstich was also heard saying he was baling out, and ended up in captivity. Hull was a long serving member of the unit and one of its aces, with five confirmed victories and one more probable – he had also been awarded the DFM. Hirstich, a young New-Zealand from Auckland was taken prisoner but his wounds were so severe that he died on the 20th. During the remainder of the month, the Squadron participated in Exercise *'Spartan'*, with no incident to report.

In March, the Squadron undertook a steadily increasing number of sorties, close to 200, with various escorts to bombers (on the 5th, 6th, and two on the 9th), and one attack on a convoy without losses on the 10th. The Squadron also flew with some Mk.VIIs, and Mk.IXs inherited from the SS Flight, allowing some pilots to test the Squadron's future machine at the same time.

In April, the introduction and use of the Mk.VII became widespread, but the Mk.VI was still the Squadron's main combat machine, and half of the sorties that month were flown on this type. In May, however, only 23 of the 157 sorties were flown on the Mk.VI. Despite this decreasing activity for the Mk.VI some accidents were reported, such as the loss of the AB211. This Mk.VI was flown by F/Sgt L.C. Haynes, who was killed after flying too low and colliding with a church building on the 26th. The last two operational Mk.VI sorties for 124 Squadron took place on the 30th when F/O G.C. Draper and Sgt L.E. Morshead took off at 19.10 on scramble, patrolled at 10,000 feet and returned one hour later without any incident to report. However training continued on that type for a while, and Sgt Morshead was killed four days later in AB503 during a cloud flying exercise. He was seen entering clouds at 8,000 feet and his aircraft was subsequently seen falling in pieces. It is presumed that the aircraft had been overstressed and broken up in the air, leaving no chance for its pilot. This loss closed the Mk.VI chapter for 124 Squadron. Contrary to its sister squadron, No. 616, the Mk.VI era was not seen as being a disastrous one, losses and claims with the type being fairly positive. However, the departure of the Mk.VI was not regretted, pilots being happy to fly the newer Mk.VII.

Exercise *Spartan* in March 1943, Spitfire Mk Vs of 421 Squadron sharing Croughton airfield with Spitfire Mk VIs of 124 Squadron (at the back). The Spitfire Mk VIs visible are ON-P, AB503/ON-N and **AB513/ON-X**. (*Andrew Thomas*)

Claims - 124 Squadron (Confirmed and Probable)

Date	Pilot	SN	Origin	Type	Serial	Code	Nb	Cat.
19.08.42	F/Sgt Peter E.G. **Durnford**	RAF No. 1254723	RAF	Fw190	**BR569**		1.0	C
				Do217	**BR569**		1.0	C
	F/L William **Gregson**	RAF No. 103520	RAF	Fw190	**BR587**	ON-T	1.0	C
	P/O Michael P. **Kilburn**	RAF No. 116807	RAF	Fw190	**BR579**	ON-H	1.0	P
	F/Sgt Bernard J. **Hull**	RAF No.1169226	RAF	Fw190	**BR319**		1.0	C
				Ju88	**BR319**		1.0	P
29.08.42	Sgt Albert M.L. **Herreman**	RAF No. 1299904	(Bel)/RAF	Fw190	**BR314**	ON-Y	1.0	C
	P/O Michael P. **Kilburn**	RAF No. 116807	RAF	Fw190	**BR579**	ON-H	1.0	C
02.10.42	P/O Peter E.G. **Durnford**	RAF No. 128994	RAF	Fw190	**BR569**		1.0	P
12.12.42	S/L Thomas **Balmforth**	RAF No. 41363	RAF	Fw190	**AB506**	ON-F	1.0	P
	P/O Bernard J. **Hull**	RAF No. 126680	RAF	Fw190	**BR598**		1.0	C
	P/O Michael P. **Kilburn**	RAF No. 116807	RAF	Fw190	**BR579**	ON-H	1.5	C
	Sgt John **Saphir**	Can./ R.110334	RCAF	Fw190	**BR987**		0.5	C

Total: 13.0

Summary of the aircraft lost on Operations - 124 Squadron

Date	Pilot	S/N	Origin	Serial	Code	Fate
19.08.42	Sgt John B. **Shanks**	RAF No. 1192260	RAF	**BR575**		PoW
19.11.42	P/O Peter E.G. **Durnford**	RAF No. 128994	RAF	**BR569**		PoW
17.02.43	F/L Frederick G.H. **Chalk**	RAF No. 81839	RAF	**AB530**	ON-Z	†
	P/O Bernard J. **Hull**	RAF No. 126680	RAF	**AB533**		†
	Sgt Bruce McK. **Hirstich**	NZ41430	RNZAF	**BR571**		†
	F/O Basil R. **Murphy**	RAF No. 119286	RAF	**AB298**		Eva.

Total: 6

Summary of the aircraft lost by accident - 124 Squadron

Date	Pilot	S/N	Origin	Serial	Code	Fate
28.09.42	Sgt James Jr. **Shea**	Can./ R.98395	RCAF	**BR587**	ON-T	†
15.10.42	Sgt Edward A. **Riseley**	RAF No. 1384159	RAF	**BR567**		-
26.05.43	F/Sgt Lawrence C. **Haynes**	RAF No. 1034417	RAF	**AB211**		†
03.06.43	Sgt Leslie E. **Morshead**	Aus. 413004	RAAF	**AB503**	ON-N	†

Total: 4

April 1942
December 1943

Victories - confirmed or probable claims: 7.0

First operational sortie: 09.05.42
Last operational sortie: 24.12.43

Number of sorties: ca. 3,370
Total aircraft written-off: 25
Aircraft lost on operations: 20
Aircraft lost in accidents: 5

Squadron code letters:
YQ

COMMANDING OFFICERS

S/L Harry L.I. Brown	RAF No. 37060	RAF	...	01.02.43
S/L Gordon S.K. Haywood	RAF No. 37879	RAF	01.02.43	04.04.43
S/L Peter W. Lefevre (s/d - Eva.)	RAF No. 40719	RAF	04.04.43	16.04.43
S/L Percy B. Lucas	RAF No. 100626	RAF	20.04.43	03.07.43
S/L Leslie W. Watts	RAF No. 117728	RAF	03.07.43	...

SQUADRON USAGE

In April 1942, 616 Squadron was the first to be chosen to fly the Mk.VI operationally. This unit had been flying the Spitfire since October 1939 and, since then, its pilots had claimed around 80 victories. It was led by S/L Brown, a very experienced pilot who had fought in Middle East with 112 Sqn. In April, pilots and crews were sent to Boscombe Down to learn about their new mounts, which began to arrive on the 22nd, while operational flights were still carried out on Mk.Vs. The clamped-on, pressurised cockpit hood was soon identified as the feature pilots disliked the most because it could not be opened in flight. The cockpit heating was also troublesome, because, while comfortable above 15,000 feet, below that altitude, the cockpit became too hot. On 9

Delivered in March 1942 to No.8 MU, AB534, seen here before its delivery to the RAF, was issued to 616 Sqn in May 1942. It was lost during the cover of Operation 'Jubilee' in August 1942.
(Peter Arnold's collection)

The Empire in action in Spring 1942: Returning from a mission, just before the Spitfire Mk.VI era, six pilots from the Empire are posing for the posterity. Left to right, 'Tess' Ware, New Zealand, who became the first 616 Sqn member to be killed on a MK.VI, 'Trapper' Bowen, Canada, who left at the end of May 1942 and later served with 403 (RCAF) Sqn , 'Johnny' Johnson, England who left in June and to become the British-top scorer, John Smithson, Australia, and Alan R. Winter, Southern Rhodesia. Winter left in October that year to serve in Malta with No.229 Sqn. (*H.A. Crafts*)

May, the Mk.VI was used for the first time operationally when two of them, along with ten Mk.Vs, were sent for a sweep over Northern France from West Malling alongside No.411 (RCAF) Squadron. The sweep flew over Gravelines and Hardelot but was uneventful, returning to base after 1h 10 min of flight. In the following days, pilots continued to practise in the Mk.VI, sometimes reaching 40,000 feet, while still flying some patrols at low level with Mk.Vs. On the 25th, the Mk.VI opened its score for the Squadron when a Do217 was intercepted. Four pilots on convoy patrol, P/O C.B. Brown, Sgt N.G. Welsh, F/L J.E. Johnson and Sgt J.H. Smithson, were called to intercept an enemy aircraft which was spotted over the Leicester area between 4,000 and 9,000 feet. All the pilots but F/L Johnson fired at the aircraft, which was claimed as damaged, and they also shared credit with one pilot of 411 Squadron. However, this first Mk.VI engagement was not one-sided as the gunners of the Dornier returned fire, hitting the plexiglass of Brown's aircraft and wounding Brown severely in the right eye. He was able to return home, but could not fly in operations any more. The next day a tragic accident occurred when P/O 'Tess' Ware, a New Zealander, lost his life while practising interception with the Polish 303 Squadron. His aircraft was seen to dive at great speed before the wings broke off, causing the Spitfire to crash and burn out, leaving no chance of survival for the pilot. It was the end of the month before the Squadron became fully operational on the Mk.VI.

June for 616 Squadron was, generally speaking, an uneventful month in terms of action against the enemy. However, on the 3rd, the Squadron first lost a pilot and an aircraft to Luftwaffe action. That day, the Squadron took off for a diversionary sweep over the Le Touquet-Boulogne area (*Circus 184*) when 12 Bf109s were seen off Cap Gris Nez. The Squadron tried to engage them without success. Sadly, an Australian pilot, P/O P.J. Moore was posted missing, believed to having been shot down. Another diversionary sweep was carried out two days later, the only other offensive mission of the month. All other sorties were uneventful patrols.

On 8 July, the Squadron moved down to Kenley to replace 485 (NZ) Sqn. However this move was short lived as it was recognised that the Squadron could not be used as a top cover squadron with satisfaction. No. 616 was the only unit flying the Mk.VI at Kenley while the others were still equipped with Mk.Vs, so no flight over 27,000 feet could have been undertaken. The short stay at Kenley was not without results though, as the Squadron was able to add to its score with the Mk.VI on 13 July. That day, an offensive sweep was planned with Nos.402 (RCAF) and 602 Sqns, with 616 Sqn flying at 22,000 feet. The pilots orbited over Abbeville and proceed south west when F/L 'Tony' Gaze, an Australian serving in the RAF, spotted a single Fw190 flying towards St-Valery. After making sure it was not a decoy, he dived down on it and shot a burst. However, this claim was accepted only a probable. Five days later, once more, it was F/L Gaze who distinguished himself. He had taken off with P/O R. Park (RAAF) to patrol Shoreham when they were told that enemy aircraft were proceeding west. They tried to find them, and eventually, half way across the Channel, Gaze spotted two Fw190s flying below him in the opposite direction. He turned round and stalked them

'Tony' Gaze from Melbourne, Australia, made the first confirmed claim on board of a Mk.VI. He ended the war awarded a DFC and 2 bars with 14 confirmed victories, 3 being shared and 4 more probable and 5 damaged and 1 V-1 destroyed.
(Gaze family)

Combat report:
F.A.G. Gaze (Australian), 18 July 1942, first Mk.VI confirmed claim.

PERSONAL COMBAT REPORT.   F/Lt. F.A.O. Gaze (Aus) DFC.   616 Squadron.

FORM "F"

FROM:-
TO:-

DATE	A. 18th July, 1942
UNIT	B. 616 Squadron.
TYPE & MARK OF OUR AIRCRAFT	C. Spitfire VI C.
TIME ATTACK WAS DELIVERED	D. 08.50.
PLACE OF ATTACK	E. 10 miles West of Le Touquet.
WEATHER	F. 10/10 at 3000ft over Channel.
OUR CASUALTIES AIRCRAFT	G. Nil.
PERSONNEL	H. Nil.
ENEMY CASUALTIES IN AIR COMBAT	J. 1 F.W. 190 destroyed. 1 F.W. 190 damaged.
ENEMY CASUALTIES GROUND OR SEA TARGETS	K. N/A.

GENERAL REPORT:

Scrambled with P/O Park, RAAF from Friston but was told that bandit had turned back and to patrol Friston - Shoreham. A few minutes later I was told that a 3 plus was to the South of me and given vector 110 buster. The huns were later reported 8 miles ahead, but as I was approaching the French coast I turned back. About half way across the Channel, flying at about 500 ft, I saw 2 aircraft, which I identified as F.W. 190s., flying in the opposite direction about 5 miles away and right down on the sea, so I turned and chased them using 14 lbs boost and managed to close in to 500 yards. The Huns were then heading towards a bank of low cloud, so I fired three short bursts of cannon at the nearest aircraft on the starboard to try and make it turn before entering cloud. Instead the two enemy aircraft started a gradual dive towards the sea, so I dived steeply to sea level and managed to get ahead of them 500 ft below the leader, who was on the port and pulled up underneath him giving a short burst of cannon and machine gun, which hit him in the belly and starboard wing. His undercarriage dropped and I gave him another burst of about 2 secs as he turned left diving towards the sea. The other 190 also turned left sharply so I followed it around and fired a burst seeing a cannon strike on the fusilage. My cannon then ran out so I fired my remaining machine gun at him with no result other than some small pieces breaking off the tail. No de Wilde strikes were seen and on landing it was found that only 25 rounds had been fired. As my tracer had gone I knew I had little ammo. left so called up my No. 2 who had now caught up and told him to chase the hun home, while I took a cine shot of the pilot of the first F.W. who had pulled up in front of me earlier in the fight and baled out at about 700 ft. I had given him a burst of machine gun as he pulled up in front of me, and as he baled out, flames poured out of the cockpit and the aircraft went straight into the sea. The pilot's parachute canopy had several large holes in it and I think he must have been wounded as he made no attempt to release himself from his parachute and was being dragged by it across the water when I left. Cine gun used.

Rounds fired: 117   20 mm cannon shell.
                1065 0.303 machine gun.
1 stoppage in Port 1 gun due to insufficient recoil. Only 25 rounds fired.

and fired almost all the Spitfire's cannon shells. The first German – Fw Klaus Oldermann of 5./JG2 – was seen to bale out, while the second was able to escape but was claimed as damaged. The successful interception was the first confirmed victory for a Spitfire Mk.VI. On the 29th, the Squadron moved to Great Stamford. The following day, the Squadron experienced its first major setback, losing four aircraft and two pilots. At this time, 124 Squadron had just followed 616 by converting onto the Mk.VI, so the two Squadrons were formed into a Wing. The Wing took off for a Ramrod mission and flew at 500 feet until reaching the Channel, then started to climb and crossed the French coast at 17,000 feet. At this point, the Squadrons were told that enemy aircraft were climbing to intercept them. They passed over Boulogne at 20,000 feet then turned for home. While 5-10 miles inland from Boulogne, they were bounced by Fw190s and Bf109s and in the ensuing melee, Kenyan-born Sgt M.H.F Cooper and P/O 'Bob' Large were hit and forced to bale out, being rescued later on. However, before he had to bale out, Large hit one of his aggressors, which he claimed as probably destroyed. Less fortunate was P/O J.R Mace, who was posted missing, while Sgt D. Lee returned to Biggin Hill with his aircraft in flames but crashed there fatally.

As for many fighter squadrons, the big event of August for No. 616 was the combined operation over Dieppe on 19th. The Squadron operated from Hawkinge and four missions were carried during the day. Even though many engagements were reported, only one confirmed victory was claimed with four further aircraft claimed as damaged – all Fw190s – for the loss of four aircraft and the South African pilot Sgt N.W.J. Coldrey during the second mission of the day. Two more Fw190s were claimed as damaged during the third mission, with the loss of F/L J.S. Fifield, who was later rescued. The rest of the month was uneventful, but the Squadron was sad to see F/L Gaze leaving the unit at the end of the month, when he took command of 64 Squadron.

On 9 September, 616 Squadron had a rare opportunity to intercept a very high flying aircraft, and while P/O P.J. Blanchard and Sgt Goodyear were able to reach 38,600 feet, they were recalled before completing the interception... at that time, the German aircraft, probably a Ju-86P, was still flying 4,000 feet above the RAF pilots! Otherwise in September and October 1942, the Squadron was based at Tangmere where it became operational from the 24th September. Standing patrols were provided regularly by the Tangmere Sector as a precaution against the fighter-bomber Fw190s which frequently raided the South coast. Before that day, the Squadron experienced little activity except when they were called to provide a top escort to USAAF Fortresses on the 6th. The standing patrols were sometimes stopped to allow the squadron to carry out other missions, such as another escort for USAAF Fortresses on the 26th, or some uneventful scrambles. On 2 October, 616 Squadron flew with 124 Squadron for a close escort to 6 US Fortresses (*Circus* 221) and on the way home, P/O Large and his wingman were involved in a dogfight in which Large claimed one aircraft destroyed. Sergeant Cooper was shot down, and forced to abandon his machine, BR159, over the Channel. Large returned to base and took another Spitfire to locate his wingman and helped a Walrus in finding him. For his action Large was awarded the DFC while for Cooper this was the second time for him to be shot down in a Mk.VI – a dubious privilege! Otherwise, even though the Squadron was involved in major operations like an escort of 108 B-17s on the 9th, nothing of note took place until the end of October.

John H. Smithson from Victoria, Australia, was serving with 616 Sqn since November 1941 when the Mk.VI was introduced into the unit in Spring 1942. He claimed two aircraft damaged during Operation 'Jubilee'. At the end of his tour in October 1942, he was repatriated to Australia and was posted to No.457 (RAAF) Sqn with which he would become one of its more successful pilots in 1944, claiming four aircraft including two at night. (*H.A. Crafts*)

On the first day of November, bad weather prevailed and only three convoy patrols were carried out, but one of these ended tragically. Having taken off at 14.15, Sgt J.K. Rodgers and Sgt P.S. Smith (RNZAF) were recalled 15 minutes later because of the deteriorating weather but both crashed into a hillside at Nettlecombe on the Isle of Wight. Sgt Smith died in the crash but Sgt Rodger owed his life to the fact that his aircraft went clean through a brick wall, thus enabling him to make a forced landing. He escaped with slight concussions and slight head injuries. While 274 sorties were flown during the month, the period was uneventful for the Squadron, mainly involving patrols. The exceptions to this were one *Ramrod* (No.22), two *Circus* (Nos.235 & 236) and three *Rhubarb* missions. December was also quiet, with 255 sorties flown, while January 1943 was even more so, with about 100 sorties flown including two *Circus* escorts for Ventura bombers and one *Ramrod*.

That month, two experienced pilots left the Squadron. P/O Large ended the tour he had started with 616 Squadron 18 months previously as a Sergeant. On 1st February S/L Brown also left, for the RAFC, relinquishing command to S/L G.SK. Haywood who had been posted as supernumerary a few days before. In February air activity resumed slowly. On 7th, 616 Squadron provided an escort for the Prime Minister's Liberator 'Commando', but on the 18th, the Squadron recorded the loss of P/O P.J. Blanchard who was killed while practising a squadron sweep. By the end of the month, serviceability fell steadily because of a lack of available replacement aircraft and spare parts. It reached the point where the pilots were informed that a possible re-equipment with Mk.Vs was being considered, something the squadron was very pleased to hear. However that never came to pass, and 616 Squadron soldiered on with the Mk.VI for a couple more months. In March, 616 Squadron participated in exercise 'Spartan', during which BR585 collided with BS453 at around 16.00. Both aircraft were later stuck off charge, but no casualties were reported. Operational flights resumed from 14 March. On 24 March, during a practice sweep flight, P/O J.K. Rodger's recently commissioned aircraft BS448 collided with the Canadian Sgt S. Fowler's aircraft, BR302, over Dorchester. Rodger baled out and landed safely and Fowler (who had been involved in a previous mid-air collision) was able to return to base. BR302 was later repaired, and returned to the squadron in August.

In April, a new Squadron commander, S/L P.W. 'Pip' Lefevre arrived, and took command on the 4th. He had been awarded the DFC in 1941 while serving with 126 Squadron in Malta. The next day, the Squadron was involved a furious combat, something which it had not experienced for months. While 616 was escorting Venturas to Brest, Fw190s appeared and shot down one of the bombers. Spitfires of 616 Squadron dived onto them while others orbited over the downed Ventura's crew, and all the while more Fw190s joined the melee. F/L P.B. Wright – who had been awarded the DFC while flying with 610 Squadron – was posted missing and another Spitfire was slightly damaged but was able to return home. During this combat, only one claimed was reported, Sgt Cooper (born in Kenya) claiming one aircraft damaged. When 30 miles south of the Lizard, another Ventura was seen going into the sea and F/L G.B. MacLachlan detached his dinghy, removed it from his pack and threw it through his clear vision panel to the four men in the water.

On the 16th, the Squadron was led for the first time by the new CO. No. 616 had been called again to escort bombers, this time American B-24s, and heavy flak was encountered during the mission. The CO's aircraft was hit and was seen diving into ground. (Lefevre survived and even evaded capture, returning to the UK in mid-July). Then, Fw190s attacked and they shot down F/L McLachalan who was killed. In return Sgt T. 'Dixie' Dean claimed one Fw190 probably destroyed. In less than two weeks, the Squadron had been severely hit, in losing its CO and two flight commanders. Bad luck was not over for the Squadron, which lost another aircraft while carrying out an Air-Sea Rescue (ASR) mission, when Sgt S.J. Fowler's aircraft encountered mechanical trouble and the engine cut. He was obliged

---

The last three 616 COs for the Spitfire Mk. VI era, all being Malta veterans of 1942, left to right, 'Pip' Lefevre, who also fought in Norway and during the Battle of Britain and led the 185 over the Island, and who was later killed as OC of No. 266 (Rhodesia) Squadron on Typhoon, 'Laddie' Lucas who led the 249 over Malta and survived the war, and 'Les' Watts fought with Nos.603 and 249 Sqns during the worst months of the Malta siege in 1942 and was able to make various claimed. For his second tour, he was posted to 616 Sqn in June 1943, then 322 (Dutch) Sqn, both as a Flight commander before returning the squadron as CO. He remained with the 616 until his death on 29.04.45 while flying a Meteor.

to ditch - his third Mk.VI mishap! He was however picked up by a Walrus later on. Two days later, the new CO, P.B. 'Laddie' Lucas arrived. Lucas was another DFC-decorated, former Malta pilot (formerly of 249 Sqn). On 20 April, F/L L.W. Watts, yet another veteran from Malta, joined as a Flight Commander, while P. Steward took over the second leaderless Flight. Without a doubt it had been a black April for 616 Squadron, with heavy losses and few claims in return in 360 sorties.

Despite maintaining a high level of readiness in May, the Squadron's activity was limited to convoy patrols, high altitude patrols and scrambles for most of the month even if the unit participated in some offensive strikes over the continent. Enemy aircraft were rarely encountered and the pilots only once had the opportunity to engage them, on the 28th, without any results. The following day, P/O J. Joubert and Sgt J.L.J. Croquet were luckier, each claiming one Fw190 damaged during a high flying patrol. In June, operations continued in this vein, but on the 15th, one pilot and his aircraft were lost during a Roadstead mission. The mission, which was led by the CO and co-ordinated with 504 Squadron, was to escort four Whirlwinds to attack small German vessels off Guernsey. During the attack P/O R.J. Sim's aircraft was badly hit by flak and caught fire. He was last seen going down towards the water with a dead propeller in a shallow dive. No. 616 lost another aircraft on the 29th, during a *Ramrod* mission when F/O A. Drew, who had joined in three weeks earlier, had to jettison his Spitfire's auxiliary tank, which hit the tail causing the Spitfire to become almost uncontrollable. However Drew was able to reach the British Isles where he could bale out safely. The lack of success against the Luftwaffe continued into July, with the exception of a single claim made by the new CO, S/L L.W. Watts who had replaced S/L P.B. Lucas earlier in the month.

The first two weeks of August were uneventful, but on the 16th, Mike Cooper (Kenya) was forced to bale out during a *Ramrod* mission. He had called up on the radio, when leaving the target, saying that his engine was running rough. He was seen to be streaming white smoke and stated that he was about to bale out, but eventually evaded capture. One week later, on the 22nd, one more Mk.VI was lost while on convoy patrol. F/Sgt R.T. Wright's engine supercharger failed, which obliged the pilot to ditch his Spitfire. Wright was later picked up by a Walrus, suffering from shock, which kept him away from the squadron for a couple of days. On the 30th 616 Squadron was able to add one more enemy aircraft to its tally, but once again, not without loss. That day was dedicated to the search of a Mustang pilot posted missing the previous day and on the third sortie, the squadron had to face to eight Fw190s. As the result, the RAF was able to claim the destruction of two of them, by W/C J.H. Charles (the Wing leader) and F/Sgt F.W. Rutherford, while F/L Steward (B Flight commander) made a claim for one more damaged. However two pilots from 616 Squadron were lost, F/Sgt R. McKillop and Sgt P.W. Shale, both being posted missing. Arguably, the only satisfying moment of the month for the pilots was the arrival of the first Spitfire Mk.VII...

With the introduction of the Mk.VII, the Mk.VI was progressively withdrawn from operations. The last months of the Mk.VI with 616 Squadron consisted of convoy patrols and uneventful scrambles. The last two Mk.VI sorties were recorded in November, on the 11th when Sgt J.C. Clarke and F/Sgt R.S. George took off on scramble at 16.55 and returning 50 minutes later with nothing to report, almost marking an end to the link between the Squadron and the Mk.VI. That operation can be seen as the last true sortie of a 616 Squadron Mk.VI, but actually one more sortie was reported later in the year. Indeed, some Mk.VI Spitfires were retained with the squadron until the end of the year, being used for training, but on the 24th December, due to lack of available Mk.VIIs, F/Sgt C.E. Prouting flew a Mk.VI while participating in an escort mission to Typhoons over France. However, Prouting had to return early to base owing to fuel tank trouble. If the association between the Mk.VI and 124 Squadron was not particularly negative, the association with No. 616 was rather worse, with close to 20 aircraft lost in operations – the majority shot down by the Luftwaffe – against 7 claims, from over 3,300 sorties. In the light of 124 Squadron's results, 616 Squadron seems to have been particularly unlucky with the Mk.VI, even if this Spitfire variant was probably not the best of the breed.

Claims - 616 Squadron (Confirmed and Probable)

Date	Pilot	SN	Origin	Type	Serial	Code	Nb	Cat.
13.07.42	F/L Frederick A.O. **Gaze**	RAF No. 60096	(AUS)/RAF	Fw190			1.0	P
18.07.42	F/L Frederick A.O. **Gaze**	RAF No. 60096	(AUS)/RAF	Fw190			1.0	C
30.07.42	P/O Ronald G. **Large**	RAF No. 113371	RAF	Fw190			1.0	P
19.08.42	F/L Frederick A.O. **Gaze**	RAF No. 60096	(AUS)/RAF	Do217			1.0	C
02.10.42	P/O Ronald G. **Large**	RAF No. 113371	RAF	Fw190		YQ-J	1.0	C
16.04.43	Sgt Thomas D. **Dean**	RAF No. 1233709	RAF	Fw190		YQ-G	1.0	P
31.08.43	Sgt Frank W. **Rutherford**	RAF No. 1497152	RAF	Fw190		YQ-S	1.0	C

Total: 7.0

Summary of the aircraft lost on Operations - 616 Squadron

Date	Pilot	S/N	Origin	Serial	Code	Fate
03.06.42	P/O Peter J. Moore	RAF No. 112401	(AUS)/RAF	BR191		†
30.07.42	P/O Ronald G. Large	RAF No. 113371	RAF	BS108		-
	Sgt Michael H.F. Cooper	RAF No. 791150	RAF	BR167		-
	P/O James R. Mace	RAF No. 118169	RAF	BR597		PoW
	Sgt Donald Lee	RAF No. 1068365	RAF	BR243		†
19.08.42	Sgt Norman W.J. Coldrey	RAF No. 778619	(SA)/RAF	AB529		†
	F/L John S. Fifield	RAF No. 83274	RAF	AB534		-
02.10.42	F/Sgt Michael H.F. Cooper	RAF No. 791150	RAF	BR159	YQ-B	-
01.11.42	Sgt Philip S. Smith	NZ413900	RNZAF	BR186	YQ-C	†
	Sgt John K. Rodger	RAF No. 1365682	RAF	BR174	YQ-A	-
05.04.43	F/L Peter B. Wright	RAF No. 119180	RAF	BS465	YQ-P	†
16.04.43	S/L Peter W. Lefevre	RAF No. 40719	RAF	BS114	YQ-C	Eva.
	F/L Gordon B. MacLachlan	RAF No. 101490	RAF	BS245	YQ-A	†
18.04.43	Sgt Stanley J. Fowler	Can./ R.102190	RCAF	BR590	YQ-F	-
15.06.43	P/O Robert J. Sim	NZ403995	RNZAF	BR319	YQ-C	†
29.06.43	F/O Anthony Drew	RAF No. 128710	RAF	BR314	YQ-X	-
16.08.43	F/O Michael H.F. Cooper	RAF No. 133025	RAF	BR987	YQ-R	Eva.
22.08.43	F/Sgt Reginald T. Wright	Aus. 412759	RAAF	BS115	YQ-V	-
31.08.43	Sgt Paul W. Shale	RAF No. 1334665	RAF	BR329	YQ-E	†
	F/Sgt Ronald McKillop	RAF No. 657687	RAF	BS117	YQ-T	†

Total: 20

Summary of the aircraft lost by accident - 616 Squadron

Date	Pilot	S/N	Origin	Serial	Code	Fate
26.05.42	P/O Leicster B. Ware	NZ404007	RNZAF	BR172		†
11.08.42	Sgt Richard H.J. Noad	RAF No. 1313945	RAF	BR164		†
18.02.43	P/O Peter J. Blanchard	RAF No. 121517	RAF	BR310	YQ-G	†
04.03.43	Sgt Stanley J. Fowler	Can./ R.102190	RCAF	BR585		-
24.03.43	P/O John K. Rodger	RAF No. 139638	RAF	BS448		-

Total: 5

With Other Fighter Units

Before the Mk.VI was withdrawn from first line units, some machines began to be used by other squadrons undergoing rest periods in Groups other than 11 and 12. In these units they were always used alongside other types, generally the Mk.V, and generally speaking little air activity was noted.

No. 66 Sqn - code LZ
Received a handful of Mk.VIs in May and June 1943 while based at Skeabrae in the Orkneys alongside Mk.Vs. Only 41 sorties on Mk.VIs were carried out, but one aircraft was lost in an accident. On 22 May, F/Sgt Hill (RAAF) was taking off for an aircraft test when the engine cut. Hill was able to make a belly landing but the aircraft was a total write-off. Hill was lucky enough to suffer only bruises.

Date	Pilot	S/N	Origin	Serial	Code	Unit	Fate
22.05.43	F/Sgt Arthur H. **Hill**	Aus. 401789	RAAF	**AB527**		66 Sqn	-

No. 91 Sqn - code DL
Six Spitfire Mk VIs seem to have been alloted to 91 during the summer of 1942 of which three are known to have flown on operations (AB527, BR304 and BR326). The other three were either never physically taken on charge either sent back after a few days at the squadron. By early September 1942 they have all gone and in all less than 50 sorties were carried out on the type.

No. 118 Sqn - code NK
Twnety-seven sorties were logged in October while based at Peterhead and Castletown in October 1943.

No. 129 Sqn - code DV
While stationed at Grimsetter, a handful of sorties (14) were flown on the Mk.VI.

No. 132 Sqn - code FF
Four sorties were logged by 132 Squadron's pilots in March 1944. The unit was based at Castletown at that time.

No. 234 Sqn - code AZ
The Mk VI was used between March and May 1943 while based at Skeabrae and Grimsetter in the Orkneys. A total of 107 sorties were flown without incident.

No. 310 (Czech) Sqn - code NN
310 Squadron flew some Mk VI Spitfires between July and September 1943 while stationed at Castletown (Northern Scotland). The Czech pilots flew regularly on this type and 137 sorties were flown without major incident.

No. 313 (Czech) Sqn - code RY
While at Peterhead (north of Aberdeen, Scotland), the 313 used some Mk.VIs as well in June-July 1943 – 71 sorties were flown in July only. No incidents were reported.

No. 421 (RCAF) Sqn - code AU
This squadron appears in the list of the units that took charge of Spitfire Mk VIs during the summer 1942. If that did so, they were not used in operations.

No. 504 Sqn - code TM
Between September 1943 and January 1944, 504 Sqn used a handful of Mk.VIs, which were concentrated in A Flight, while based at Castletown then Peterhead. No. 504 continued to carry out training flights on the Mk VI until the Mk IX arrived to replace the Mk Vs and Mk VIs. Only 58 sorties were flown on the Mk.VI.

No. 602 Sqn - code LO
Another unit which used the Mk.VI while based at Skeabrae between September and November 1942. Twenty-two sorties were flown in September and 13 in November – no details are given for October, though the number of sorties must have remained very low.

Some Station Flights on bases where the Mk.VI was located used one or two Mk.VIs, such as Peterhead or Castletown, and even Northolt. In addition, the High Altitude Flight used at least two Mk.VI Spitfires, including BR318 and BR326, when it was formed in September 1942. They were used with other types of Spitfire dedicated to high altitude flight, the Mk.VII and Mk.IX, in the hope of catching the Ju-86P. The flight was re-designated the Sub-Stratosphere Flight (SS Flight) and was absorbed by 124 Sqn on 24.01.43. By that time only BR326 was still flying with the flight, BR318 having been sent to 616 Squadron in October 1942.

With The Meteorological Units

The Spitfire Mk.VI was found to be useful for the RAF's meteorological reconnaissance units. Around 16 Spitfire Mk.VIs were used by Met Squadrons or Flights, the main one being 519 Squadron, which used eight of them between August 1943 and November 1944. They were used to carry on PRATA flights (PRessure And Temperature Ascent) and all had their armament deleted. As for 519 Squadron, over 550 of such flights were flown by Spitfire Mk.VI, usually one per day, but this number was doubled around D-Day and the following weeks up to and including September. The other units which received one or more Mk.VIs were: No.521 Sqn, and Nos.1401, 1402 and 1406 Flights. Some accident were recorded, first when BR171, flown by the Canadian pilot W/O L.G. Wilson had to abandon his aircraft over the Moray Firth during a PRATA flight on 15.10.43 after his engine had caught fire, but Wilson was never found. A couple of weeks later, F/Sgt R. Johsnon was posted missing after having taken off at 14.10. He was last heard at 14.29 when being 30 miles east of Duncansby Head at 24,000 feet. Early in 1945, the RAF decided to withdrawn from use the last Mk.VIs still flying with the Met units for subsequent scrapping. It is during a ferry flight to a Maintenance unit the last loss of a Mk.VI was recorded. On 10 February 1945, the pilot of EN176 was taxying in cross wind on very soft grass verge when the aircraft swung off perimeter track due to gust wind. The wheels sank in soft turf and the Spitfire tipped on nose and was damaged in the process. Of course, even repairable, no repairs were carry on and EN176 was struck off charge at once.

Date	Pilot	S/N	Origin	Serial	Code	Unit	Fate
15.10.43	W/O Lloyd G. **Wilson**	Can./ R.54332	RCAF	**BR171**	M	519 Sqn	†
18.04.44	F/Sgt Reginald **Johnson**	RAF No. 1575601	RAF	**BR599**	W	519 Sqn	†
10.02.45	First Officer K.H.V. **Day**	-	ATA	**EN176**		3. FP	-

In The Middle East

At the end of summer 1942, the radar stations on the Suez Canal were regularly detecting reconnaissance aircraft flying at around 40,000 feet. With the military situation on the ground and with preparations underway for what would later be called the Battle of El Alamein, this was very concerning and a solution had to be found urgently. One of these was to send a small number of Spitfire Mk VI aircraft to the region. Six, from among the last Mk VI Spitfires built (BS106, BS124, BS133, BS134, BS149 and BS427), were shipped out between September 1942 and the end of October 1942, and a special high altitude flight was formed within No.103 Maintenance Unit at Aboukir, Egypt. This was done to try to intercept the Junkers Ju-86P-2 reconnaissance aircraft which were flying sometimes as high as 50,000 ft. However, the Mk.VI proved to be unsuitable for this task, mainly because of its pressurisation system which seemed to be too heavy, and thus rendered the Spitfires unable to reach the Junkers' altitude. The use of the Mk.VI as fighter was consequently short-lived and the Mk.VIs were eventually replaced with a locally modified Mk.V variant which gave more satisfactory performance.

After that, the career of the Mk.VI in Middle East became limited, partially due to the recurrent problem of spare parts supply, as with the Mk.VIs serving in the UK. However, three found their way to a reconnaissance unit, 680 Sqn, based in the area. Two were taken on charge in March 1943, these being BS106 and BS149. They were first used to train pilots for aircraft with pressurised cockpits, but actually few flights were recorded. While BS106 is believed to have been used as a trainer only, BS149 is known to have been modified as a fighter reconnaissance aircraft with F.8 oblique camera installed, probably without wing armament. Two operational flights were carried out, the first on 17.03.43 by F/O R.L. Westinghouse, and the second on 15.04.43 by P/O J. Lowe who crash-landed on his return. The aircraft was sent away for repairs and was replaced by BS133, also modified. Another reconnaissance mission was carried out on 3 May, but this was the last reconnaissance flight recorded by a Mk VI. From that point, BS106 and BS133 were used a communication aircraft, probably without any camera or armament installed until they were sent to No.103 MU for subsequent allocation. BS133 was sent back on 28.07.43, BS106 shortly after a last communication flight recorded on 2 August. Nothing much is known about their use after that date until their official date of withdrawal. BS106 was struck off charge on 26.04.45, as were BS133 and BS149. It is not clear if BS149 was repaired or flew again after its accident, and it may have been used for spare parts for the remaining Mk.VIs. BS134 is known to have flown with No. 73 OTU and was stuck off charge on 29.08.46, but as no reliable records for the Middle East are available it is possible that this could only an administrative transcription, while the aircraft had actually been scrapped a long time previously. BS124, the last of the batch sent in Middle East also served at No. 73 OTU at Fayid, but was lost in a flying accident on 13.09.44. That day, its Polish pilot, F/O Władysław L. Ślósarski – who later served with No.318 (Polish) Squadron in Italy – took off for a formation exercise but a tyre burst on take-off. The pilot completed his exercise but on return was ordered to make a wheels-up landing, marking an end to the career of BS124. This Spitfire was previously used by No. 417 (RCAF) Squadron in November and December 1942 until being damaged in a flying accident on 12 December. However, no operational flight was recorded. BS427 is also known to have served with 73 OTU but no details are available.

Date	Pilot	S/N	Origin	Serial	Code	Unit	Fate
13.09.44	F/O Władysław L. **Ślósarski**	PAF P-1924	PAF	**BS124**		73 OTU	-

BS124 while in service with No. 417 (RCAF) Squadron fitted with the large Vokes dust-proof filter. At the end of 1942, 417 was flying on Hurricanes with a handful of Spitfire Mk Vs. Serving as a fighter in the Middle east area at the end of 1942 it was painted with standard paints, Dark Earth/Middle Stone and probably Azule blue undersurfaces. The red spinner is a marking used fy the fighter in the Mediterranean at that time. (*via Malcolm Laird*)

Above, 3/4 front view of BS124 being prepared for another flight. (*via Malcolm Laird*)
Below, a photo believed to have been taken at Aboukir, Egypt, where No.103 Maintenance Unit was located. In the foreground, is probably a Spitfire Mk.VI which can be identified with its pointed wing tips and the rounded triangular opening window in the port side of the windscreen. Note the absence of any armament in the wings. (*via Malcolm Laird*)

SIMPLIFIED REGISTER

Serial	month of delivery	Squadron
AB176	Feb.42	-
AB200	Jan.42	124
AB211	Feb.42	616, 124
AB498	Feb.42	421, 91, 124
AB503	Jan.42	616, 124 *(ON-N)*
AB506	Feb.42	124 *(ON-F)*, 616
AB513	Feb.42	124 *(ON-X)*, 616
AB516	Feb.42	124 *(ON-S)*, 616
AB523	Feb.42	124, 616
AB527	Feb.42	421, 91 *(DL-J)*, 164, 602, 129, 234, 66
AB528	Feb.42	124
AB529	Apr.42	421, 616
AB530	Mar.42	124 *(ON-Z)*
AB533	Apr.42	91, 124
AB534	Mar.42	616
BR159	Mar.42	616 *(YQ-B)*
BR162	Mar.42	616, 124 *(ON-F)*, 616
BR164	Mar.42	616
BR167	Mar.42	616
BR171	Mar.42	421, 91, 124, 616, 124 *(ON-N)*, 1406 Flt, 519
BR172	Apr.42	616
BR174	Mar.42	616 *(YQ-A)*
BR178	Mar.42	616, 124, 616, 519
BR181	Mar.42	616, 124
BR186	Mar.42	616 *(YQ-C)*
BR189	Feb.42	616, 124, 310, 504
BR191	Mar.42	616
BR193	Mar.42	616, 124 *(ON-G)*, 616
BR197	Apr.42	616, 504
BR200	Apr.42	616
BR205	Apr.42	-
BR243	Apr.42	616
BR247	Apr.42	616
BR250	Apr.42	616
BR252	Apr.42	616, 602, 129, 234, 66, 313, 310, 504
BR255	Apr.42	616 *(YQ-U)*
BR286	Apr.42	616, 1402 Flt
BR287	Apr.42	521, 1401 Flt
BR289	Apr.42	616
BR297	Apr.42	164, 602, 129, 234, 66, 313, 310, 504
BR298	Apr.42	164, 602, 1402 Flt
BR302	May.42	616
BR304	Apr.42	421, 91 *(DL-Z)*, 164, 602, 129, 234, 310, 504
BR307	May.42	616, 519
BR309	May.42	616, 519
BR310	May.42	616 *(YQ-G)*
BR314	May.42	124 *(ON-Y)*, 616 *(YQ-X)*
BR318	May.42	91, 421, 616 *(YQ-L)*
BR319	May.42	124, 616 *(YQ-C)*
BR326	Apr.42	421, 91 *(DL-Q)*, 124, 616
BR329	May.42	421, 124 *(ON-R)*, 616 *(YQ-E)*
BR330	May.42	616
BR563	May.42	616, 124 *(ON-S)*, 616

BR567	May.42	**421, 124**
BR569	May.42	**124**
BR571	May.42	**154, 124**
BR575	May.42	**124**
BR577	May.42	**164, 602, 129, 234, 66, 313, 310, 504**
BR578	Jun.42	**124, 616** *(YQ-J)*
BR579	May.42	**124** *(ON-H)*, **234, 66, 313, 310, 504**
BR585	Jun.42	**91, 124** *(ON-T)*, **616**
BR587	Jun.42	**124** *(ON-T)*
BR588	Jun.42	**124** *(ON-E)*, **616** *(YQ-D)*
BR590	Jun.42	**124, 616** *(YQ-F)*
BR593	Jun.42	**124**
BR595	Jun.42	**124, 616**
BR597	Jun.42	**616**
BR598	Jun.42	**616, 124, 616, 1401 Flt**
BR599	Jun.42	**616, 519**
BR979	Jun.42	**164, 602, 234, 616**
BR983	Jul.42	**616, 521, 1401 Flt**
BR984	Jul.42	**421, 616**
BR987	Jul.42	**421, 124, 616** *(YQ-R)*
BS106	Jul.42	*Shipped to the ME*
BS108	Jul.42	**616**
BS111	Jul.42	**616** *(YQ-P)*, **1406 Flt, 519**
BS114	Jul.42	**616** *(YQ-C)*
BS115	Jul.42	**616** *(YQ-V)*
BS117	Jul.42	**616** *(YQ-T)*
BS124	Jul.42	*Shipped to the ME*
BS133	Aug.42	*Shipped to the ME*
BS134	Aug.42	*Shipped to the ME*
BS141	Aug.42	**602, 234, 66, 313, 310, 118**
BS146	Aug.42	**602, 129, 234, 313, 310, 504, 1401 Flt**
BS149	Aug.42	*Shipped to the ME*
BS228	Oct.42	**521, 1401 Flt**
BS245	Oct.42	**124, 616** *(YQ-A)*
BS427	Aug.42	*Shipped to the ME*
BS436	Sep.42	**602**
BS437	Sep.42	**602, 129, 234, 66, 313, 310, 504, 1401 Flt**
BS442	Sep.42	**602, 129, 234, 66, 313, 310, 504**
BS448	Oct.42	**616**
BS453	Oct.42	**616**
BS460	Oct.42	**616** *(YQ-S)*, **1401 Flt**
BS465	Oct.42	**616** *(YQ-P)*
BS472	Oct.42	**602, 129, 234, 66, 313, 310, 504**
EN176	Nov.42	**1402 Flt**
EN189	Nov.42	**124, 616**

IN MEMORIAM
Spitfire Mk.VI

Name	Service No	Rank	Age	Origin	Date	Serial
Blanchard, Peter James	RAF No. 121517	F/O	21	RAF	18.02.43	BR310
Chalk, Frederick Gerald Hudson	RAF No. 81389	F/L	28	RAF	17.02.43	AB530
Coldrey, Norman William Jacobus	RAF No. 778619	Sgt	26	(SA)/RAF	19.08.42	AB529
Haynes, Lawrence Charles	RAF No. 146109	P/O	20	RAF	26.05.43	AB211
Hirstich, Bruce Mackenzie	NZ41430	Sgt	20	RNZAF	20.02.43	BR571
Hull, Bernard John	RAF No. 126860	F/O	22	RAF	17.02.43	AB533
Johnson, Reginald	RAF No. 1575601	F/Sgt	29	RAF	18.04.44	BR599
Lee, Donald	RAF No. 1068365	Sgt	n/k	RAF	30.07.42	BR243
MacLachlan, Gordon Baird	RAF No. 101490	F/L	21	RAF	16.04.43	BS245
McKillop, Ronald	RAF No. 657687	F/Sgt	23	RAF	31.08.43	BS117
Moore, Peter John	RAF No. 112401	P/O	22	(AUS)/RAF	03.06.42	BR191
Morshead, Leslie Ernest	Aus. 413004	F/Sgt	21	RAAF	03.06.43	AB503
Noad, Richard Harold John	RAF No. 1313945	Sgt	19	RAF	11.08.42	BR162
Shale, Paul William	RAF No. 1334665	Sgt	20	RAF	31.08.43	BR329
Shea, James Jr.	Can./ R.98395	Sgt	19	RCAF	28.09.42	BR587
Sim, Robert James	NZ403995	F/O	23	RNZAF	15.06.43	BR319
Smith, Philip Shaw	NZ413900	Sgt	22	RNZAF	01.11.42	BR186
Ware, Leicester Bond	NZ404007	P/O	26	RNZAF	26.05.42	BR172
Wilson, Lloyd George	Can./ J.18876	P/O	23	RCAF	15.10.43	BR171
Wright, Peter Beresford	RAF No. 119180	F/L	22	RAF	05.04.43	BS465

Total: 20

Australia: 2, Canada: 2, New Zealand: 4, South Africa: 1, Uninted Kingdom: 11

n/k: not known

Supermarine Spitfire Mk. VI BR579
No. 124 (Baroda) Squadron
Pilot Officer Michael P. 'Slim' KILBURN
Debden (UK), summer 1942

Supermarine Spitfire Mk. VI AB513
No. 124 (Baroda) Squadron
Exercise Spartan
Croughton (UK), March 1943

Supermarine Spitfire Mk. VI/trop BS124
No. 417 (RCAF) Squadron
Idku (Egypt), November 1942

SQUADRONS! - The series

1. The Supermarine Spitfire Mk VI
2. The Republic Thunderbolt Mk I
3. The Supermarine Spitfire Mk V in the Far East
4. The Boeing Fortress Mk I
5. The Supermarine Spitfire Mk XII
6. The Supermarine Spitfire Mk VII
7. The Supermarine Spitfire F. 21
8. The Handley-Page Halifax Mk I
9. The Forgotten Fighters
10. The NA Mustang IV in Western Europe
11. The NA Mustang IV over the Balkans and Italy
12. The Supermarine Spitfire Mk XVI - *The British*
13. The Martin Marauder Mk I
14. The Supermarine Spitfire Mk VIII in the Southwest Pacific - *The British*
15. The Gloster Meteor F.I & F.III
16. The NA Mitchell - *The Dutch, Poles and French*
17. The Curtiss Mohawk
18. The Curtiss Kittyhawk Mk II
19. The Boulton Paul Defiant - *day and night fighter*
20. The Supermarine Spitfire Mk VIII in the Southwest Pacific - *The Australians*
21. The Boeing Fortress Mk II & Mk III
22. The Douglas Boston and Havoc - *The Australians*
23. The Republic Thunderbolt Mk II
24. The Douglas Boston and Havoc - *Night fighters*
25. The Supermarine Spitfire Mk V - *The Eagles*
26. The Hawker Hurricane - *The Canadians*
27. The Supermarine Spitfire Mk V - *The 'Bombay' squadrons*
28. The Consolidated Liberator - *The Australians*
29. The Supermarine Spitfire Mk XVI - *The Dominions*
30. The Supermarine Spitfire Mk V - *The Belgian and Dutch squadrons*
31. The Supermarine Spitfire Mk V - *The New-Zealanders*
32. The Supermarine Spitfire Mk V - *The Norwegians*
33. The Brewster Buffalo
34. The Supermarine Spitfire Mk II - *The Foreign squadrons*
35. The Martin Marauder Mk II
36. The Supermarine Spitfire Mk V - *The Special Reserve squadrons*
37. The Supermarine Spitfire Mk XIV - *The Belgian and Dutch squadrons*
38. The Supermarine Spitfire Mk II - *The Rhodesian, Dominion & Eagle squadrons*
39. The Douglas Boston and Havoc - *Intruders*
40. The North American Mustang Mk III over Italy and the Balkans (Pt-1)
41. The Bristol Brigand
42. The Supermarine Spitfire Mk V - *The Australians*
43. The Hawker Typhoon - *The Rhodesian squadrons*
44. The Supermarine Spitfire F.22 & F.24
45. The Supermarine Spitfire Mk IX - *The Belgian and Dutch squadrons*
46. The North American & CAC Mustang - *The RAAF*
47. The Westland Whirlwind
48. The Supermarine Spitfire Mk XIV - *The British squadrons*
49. The Supermarine Spitfire Mk I - *The beginning (the Auxiliary squadrons)*
50. The Hawker Tempest Mk V - *The New Zealanders*
51. The Last of the Long-Range Biplane Flying Boats
52. The Supermarine Spitfire Mk IX - *The Former Canadian Homefront squadrons*
53. The Hawker Hurricane Mk I & Mk II - *The Eagle squadrons*
54. The Hawker biplane fighters
55. The Supermarine Spitfire Mk IX - *The Auxiliary squadrons*
56. The Hawker Typhoon - *The Canadian squadrons*
57. The Douglas SBD - *New Zealand and France*
58. The Forgotten Patrol Seaplanes
59. The Dutch Fighter Squadrons - *Nos. 322 & 120 (NEI) Squadrons*
60. The Supermarine Spitfire - *The Australian Squadrons in Western Europe and the Med*
61. The Belgian Fighter Squadrons - *Nos. 349 & 350 Squadrons*
62. The Supermarine Spitfire Mk I - *The beginning (the Regular squadrons)*
63. The Hawker Typhoon - *The 'Fellowship of the Bellows' squadrons*
64. The North American Mustang Mk I & Mk II
65. The Eagle Squadrons - *Nos. 71, 121 & 133 Squadrons*
66. The Handley Page Hampden - *Toperdo-bomber*

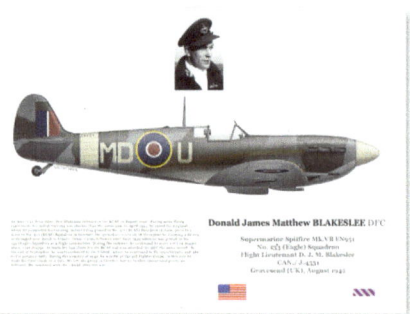

Introducing's RAF In Combat and Bravo Bravo Aviation's collection of highly-detailed and historically accurate, high-quality aviation prints. For more information on available prints, please visit:

 or

Prints in connection with this book:

PL-071: M.P. Kilburn
PL-130: J.C. Nelson

www.ingramcontent.com/pod-product-compliance
Lightning Source LLC
Chambersburg PA
CBHW060823090426
42738CB00002B/89